W9-AGB-105

My First Story of Christmas

TIM DOWLEY

Illustrated by ROGER LANGTON

Copyright © 2003 Lion Hudson
plc/Tim Dowley & Peter Wyart
trading as Three's Company

First published in the USA 2004
by Moody Publishers

Worldwide co-edition produced by
Lion Hudson plc,
Mayfield House, 256 Banbury Road
Oxford OX2 7DH, England

Tel: +44 (0) 1865 302750
Fax: +44 (0) 1865 302757
e-mail: coed@lionhudson.com
www.lionhudson.com

ISBN 0 8024 1758-2

Printed in Singapore

Moody Publishers, a ministry of the
Moody Bible Institute, is designed
for education, evangelization, and
edification. If we may assist you in
knowing more about Christ and the
Christian life, please write us without
obligation:

Moody Publishers, c/o MLM,
Chicago, Illinois 60610 USA

Long ago, in the time of King Herod of Judea,
there was a girl called Mary.
She lived in a little village in the hills.

One day God sent the
angel Gabriel to Mary.
"Don't be afraid!" he said.
"God is pleased with you."

"God is going to give you
a very special baby," said the angel.
"You must call him Jesus!"

Then the Angel
disappeared.
But Mary was very happy.
She sang a song to thank God.

Mary married Joseph, the village carpenter.
They began to get ready for the baby.

It was almost time for Mary's baby to be born.
Then the governor of the country decided
to count all the people.

So Mary and Joseph had to go
on a long journey, to a town called
Bethlehem, to be counted.

When at last they arrived in Bethlehem,
Mary was very tired.
They knocked at the
door of an inn.

"No room!" said the man.
So they had to sleep in a stable.

That night, with the donkey and cows standing close,
Mary's baby boy, Jesus, was born.

In fields nearby,
shepherds were looking after their sheep.

Suddenly an angel appeared.
The shepherds were scared.
"Don't be afraid!" said the angel.

"Tonight a special baby has been born in Bethlehem.
He will save his people."

Then crowds of angels filled the sky, singing,

"Praise God in heaven!"

The angels disappeared as quickly as they had come. All was dark again.

The shepherds rushed off into Bethlehem. They had to find the new baby!

The shepherds soon found Mary and Joseph
in the stable – and baby Jesus lying in a manger.

At the time that Jesus was born,
in a far country wise men
were looking at the night sky.

"Look!" said one. "I've never seen that new star before."

"It means a new king has been born,"
said a second.

"We must follow the star and find him,"
said the third wise man.

So the wise men set out on a long, hard journey,
following the star by night.

When they arrived in Judea, they went
straight to King Herod's palace.
But the new king Jesus was not there.

At last the star stopped over Bethlehem.

As soon as they saw little Jesus,
the wise men knelt down.

They knew he was the new king.
They gave him rich presents: gold, frankincense, and myrrh.

Each year we remember that first Christmas,
when Jesus was born in a stable.

We give each other presents,
just as the wise men gave presents to Jesus.
And just as God sent Jesus as the best gift of all.